THE RAVEN FLIES AT MIDNIGHT

Blackbird Poet

Copyright © 2016 by Blackbird Poet
All rights reserved.
Cover Design by Kat Savage
of Savage Hart Book Services
Edited by Christina Hart
of Savage Hart Book Services
Layout and Arrangement by Blackbird Poet
Interior Art Illustrations by Tanja Weidenbörner

ISBN-13: 978-1539536390
ISBN-10: 1539536394

For my husband, Greg—my friend, my muse—you have made this all possible. You showed me that despite all the turmoil, we have strength in unity. And for my children, Aidan & Jilian, you inspire me to be a better person not only for you, but for myself. You have both been my guiding light the moment you came into my life.

CONSUMED IN THE SHADOWS

Tanja Weidenbörner "Solution"

BAGGAGE CLAIM

Some of us
carry our baggage
like the homeless
and some of us
pretend we're
always on vacation.

TAKE CONTROL

We had it all
figured out
the second time,
until you let
the devil
take the wheel.

FALLING

Some of us
are just one
heartbreak away
from falling
over the edge.

HAUNTED

I wanted to free
myself from
the skeletons
in my closet
that held me hostage,
but instead
I allowed
them to haunt me
every night
as I clenched
onto my pillow.

LET ME BREATHE

I still have
moments
where breathing is a
chore and anxiety is
sitting on my chest,
but my struggles are
a part of me,
a part of my story,
and without them
I wouldn't know how
to keep going.

MAKING SENSE

I wanted to start
over with a clean slate
but the scenes of him leaving
me kept replaying in my mind.
They were
seared permanently
and would haunt me
every step of the way.
So I stayed to bear
the mess, and
waited until
the weight of it all
would crush some
sense into me.

WORLDS APART

I wish I could
understand
your deceit
and how
it has undermined
the love you say
you have for me,
but you are in your
own world and I'm
slowly fading into mine.

UNRAVEL

I allow myself
to unravel,
like a
knitted sweater,
taken apart
for salvation.

IN MY SHOES

You don't need
to walk a mile
in my shoes to
know my pain;
just look into my
eyes and you can see
right through me.
All the years
filled with screams
echoing in the hallways
and the nights
I spent alone in our bed.

BEAUTY

She could only endure
looking at her body in the
mirror if she could
see her bones—
it was the only way
she thought she
looked beautiful.

EXPOSED

I watch more
fragments of me
go as they dance
with the wind,
leaving me exposed
to all the elements
that are slowly
withering me away.

SECRETS

There is a chasm
in my chest that
keeps all my dirty
little secrets.
The bits of my
innocence that
were taken away
so easily, so forcibly,
without any regard
that I may have
needed them
to mask me from
the terrors that
would haunt me
every night.

TAKE

I want to love
you with every fiber
that I have but
sometimes I just don't
know how to.
Maybe, just maybe,
it's because the man
before you took
all the love from me
in order to keep
himself warm at night.

NO SWEAT

You sought after me
through uncharted
waters and I
allowed you to ride
my waves too willingly.

ADDICTIONS

It would
be so much
easier
to be
addicted to
something
rather than
someone.

KNOTS

I don't know
if I'm madly
in love with you
anymore,
yet the thought
of losing you
has me in knots
that I can't untie.

PIECES

You planted yourself
in my heart and
your roots
have overgrown me.
They have broken off parts
of me that I need
to survive the days
I am weak.

IDENTITY

I lost my mind
somewhere between
loving you
and burying
who I wanted to be.

IMMUNE

You took the time
to peel back my
layers but when
you left, I was an
open wound. I'm
still healing,
scabbing, and
not yet entirely
immune to you.

WISHBONE

You showed me what
love really looked like
and I succumbed to it.
But I was blindsided,
split in half
like a wishbone,
and left wondering
where I went wrong.

ILLUSIONS

Love has the ability
to fall on deaf ears,
to blind you from
what is true,
to feel with a heart
that gives relentlessly,
and to think with a
clouded mind.
We all get awed
by its illusions.

NONSENSE

How much longer
should we continue
to play these games
of love and destruction?
How much longer
should we accept broken
promises followed by
broken apologies?
This soul is worn and
cannot decide how
much longer it can withstand
the nonsense of it all.

SELFISH

Men like you run
in herds
and do not
tread lightly
on women
like me.
There's no love
for me left
after you have
filled yourself
with so much
of it.

SPOTLIGHT

He is
no longer
in the spotlight
of my life.

APOLOGIES

When the hurt
is too deep,
you can't
wash it
away with
apologies.

BLENDING IN

Some days
I just want
to blend in
with life's
backdrop.

REMEMBRANCE

This skin remembers
everyone who has
touched it, even those
who were unwelcome.

EMPTY WORDS

He continued to
feed me empty
words and I was full
but I was not satisfied.
My stomach ached
and each lie was another
wall between us that
I didn't have the
strength to break down.

BREAKING

You didn't break
my heart when
you left.
No, my dear,
you catapulted it
into oblivion.

UNEASE

My hands
may be steady
but my heart
quivers incessantly.
There is no more
comfort in this body.

ALL-CONSUMING

He consumed
my heart,
piece by piece,
so no one else
could love it.

PRISONER

I can no longer
be a slave
to my heart,
these shackles
have dug too deep
and bloody trails
cannot continue
to follow me.

DRIFTING

No matter how
many steps we
take forward,
we continue to
drift apart.

SILENCE

I've been lost
for some time now,
not knowing where
I belong in this world.
The answer may be
within, but there is
no sound, just silence
that I can't seem to break.

THE PAST

You will remain
the ache in my heart
as long as my mind
can still see
glimpses of how
we used to be.

MESS

The roughness
around my edges
may make me
heartless
at times, but I do it to
protect the frail mess
inside from getting out.

LAST GOODBYE

You left me
when darkness
filled the skies,
and now,
every night,
I'm reminded
of the loneliness
I felt inside
while I wept my
last tears for you
as I said
our last goodbye.

TAME

My heart has been
surrounded by coldness
for so long,
I've forgotten how to
love with passion.
I've tamed it
so the chaos
can be managed.
So the love
won't hurt anymore.

BUILDING WALLS

Brick by brick,
I continue to build
my walls
to protect me
when the hurt
tries to get in.
It becomes more
difficult,
as the walls
become higher,
to see any light at all.

FORGIVENESS

The guilt you carry
has been drowning us
for far too long and
I cannot bear the weight
any longer.
Forgive yourself.
The ocean is much
more cold and
unforgiving than I.

KINDNESS

I'm not a doormat
or a revolving door,
waiting with arms
wide open
at your disposal.
Don't confuse
my kindness
with naïveté.
The pot hasn't
boiled over yet
for it to burn.

SHARING WATER DURING SUNSETS

Tanja Weidenbörner "Last Embracement"

TAKEN

You had me
before our
first hello.
You'll have
me until our
last goodbye.

QUEST

Trace the freckles
on my body with
your tongue like you're
connecting constellations
as my moans guide you
on your quest.
Explore me,
exhaust me,
consume me.

NATIVE TONGUE

You spoke to me
in your native tongue
and sent my body
to regions of the
world I hadn't explored.

TASTE

Your taste
is like
my favorite
red wine,
silky smooth
with a
lingering finish.

DEEP ROOTS

I want our bodies
to entwine like
deep seeded
roots and our
minds to get lost
in the rhythm of
our beating hearts.

FIRST NIGHT

When our eyes met
for the first time,
the planets aligned,
the stars shined bright,
and the cosmic energy
vibrated around us.
You made the world
bearable that
unforgettable night.

STORM

I'm an
unpredictable storm
with
devastating results
and
you've stood
your ground,
blow
by
blow.

CHOSEN

There may not
be just one person
for us, but we
chose each other
from hundreds upon
thousands of people
and I'll choose you
again and again.

BUTTERFLIES

I used to miss
the butterflies
that I would get
when I'd hear your
voice telling me
goodnight. But now,
it's been replaced
by your
whispers telling me
that you cannot
imagine being
anywhere else but
here, lying next to me.

HOPEFUL

You could give me
a hundred heartbreaks
and I still wouldn't forget
the way you look at me
with hopeful eyes
or take my breath away
with every kiss.

GROWING OLD TOGETHER

I want the kind of love
that when I get too
old to care for myself,
you'll be there every step
of the way, helping me.
The kind of love that when
I ask you the same questions
over and over again, you
will be patient with me.
The kind of love that
when I forget your name
or who you are, you will
stay by my side to remind me.

SIDE BY SIDE

There are days
I cannot fathom
loving myself,
but here
you are,
by my side,
coaching me,
supporting me,
and
loving all the parts
of me
I want to hide.

DECISIONS OF THE HEART

I was to roam
this world alone
and free but
my heart made
the decision
to love you
indefinitely.

STILL HERE

I have
witnessed all
your demons in
their flesh,
yet here I stand.

SOFTER

I will scratch at this
hard shell
until my fingernails
bleed before I give up
on us.
I know I need
to be softer
in order to love you.

GUILT

My love, stop
carrying your guilt
like armor. I have
forgiven you but
you have yet to
forgive yourself.

HIDE NO MORE

I don't know if we
can ever truly
understand each other.
We've simply chipped
away at each other's edges.
Sometimes, I even struggle
to understand myself.
I'm hoping patience will
reveal what
we've been hiding all along.

ENTANGLED

I knew from the
moment you stole
my gaze, I would
have my heart broken,
put back together,
and forever
entangled with you.

DEEPER

He loves me,
for I'm not
afraid to
pull back
the skin
and look
underneath.

DON'T LET GO

Every moment spent
in your arms feels
like I'm losing myself
senselessly with no
need of ever wanting
my feet to touch
the ground.
I'll continue to hold
on tight if you
continue to tell
me you won't let go.

TRUTH

You stumbled
upon my feet
as if you had been
lost all this time,
but found your
truth in me.

MY LUCKY CHARM

There's something
about love that
makes everything
seem possible,
where every
adventure feels
attainable and you
feel like you're in
a dream that
never ends.
I feel lucky
to still have that
with you.

TILL DEATH DO US PART

You're born
needing someone
and when
you're dying,
you need someone.
So, when that
time comes for me
to breathe
my last breath,
I want that someone
to be you.

MEMORIES

Lovers past
have been
swept away,
like dust,
hidden but
never forgotten
as we set forth
on an adventure
of a lifetime,
where growing old
is as rare as
a shooting star,
where wrinkled skin
has folds of cherished
memories I long
to make with you.

REASONS WE LOVE

Just when I think
all the hope I have
in us is beginning
to disappear,
you show me the
many reasons why
this heart cannot
survive without you.

ATTENTION

Our love
does not
need
an audience.
But I, on the
other hand,
am starving
for your attention.

YOUR TOUCH

My heart
had hardened
with every
lie, but
you softened
it with
every embrace.

ENDURE

Sometimes, I don't
understand how we
manage to love
each other.
The gritty, raw,
ravenous memories
that fill our minds
are often the
toughest to endure.
But we do endure them,
each day, regardless of
how painful that might be.

TREASURES

Long ago
stood a
wounded girl
and a lost boy,
not knowing how
to love each other.
Years later, they
picked up each other's
pieces and treated
them as treasures.

I'LL FLY ALONE IF I HAVE TO

Tanja Weidenbörner "Awakening"

MORE

I break
only to
be built
back up
for more.

ATTENTION

I was never one
with many words,
but my actions
spoke louder and
with emotion
only felt
by those
paying attention.

UNFILTERED

I like the broken, the raw,
the condemned, the outcasts,
the quirky ones that challenge
me mentally and don't just
talk about the day to day
banter, only scratching
at the surface. Let's go deep.
I want to know what
keeps you up at night.
Give it to me, unfiltered.

MY GUIDING LIGHT

I am beginning
to shed the
years of self-abuse
that I have
been consumed
in for so long,
and I can finally see
a ray of light
peeking through.

GENTLE

Be gentle—
underneath this skin
lies someone
ready to love you
wholeheartedly.

RESILIENCE

It amazes me
how resilient
this tattered old
heart can be,
despite how much
pain it has endured.
Yet it still
manages to give
out so much love.

ACTIONS

I may not be
the type to
shower you
with affection,
but when I do,
my actions
will speak
louder than
any "I love you"
whispered.

IN CONTROL

There's always been a
little voice in my head,
telling me I'm not good enough,
telling me I'm always wrong,
telling me I'm fat and ugly.
I've learned that whether it's
true or not,
I'm the only one
who can hear it and
I'm the only one
who can shut it off.

COLD-HEARTED

The blood that
seeps from me
is warm
and assures me
I'm not
entirely
cold-hearted.

THOUGHTS

Night after night,
I chase my thoughts
and wrangle them
in my notebook,
as though they are
stray cats,
trying to
escape me.

RISE

I was born
to rise
from the ashes,
not to
choke on them.

SELF-LOVE

I was knee deep
in desperation
and hungry for advice
on how to fix what
was broken.
Then, I realized,
I wasn't the one that
needed fixing,
I just needed to
love myself.

DEPTH WITHIN

There is depth
beyond my hazel eyes,
beyond my frizzy hair
that's always kept in a bun,
beyond my delicate mouth that's
home to a sharp tongue,
and beyond my small frame
that doesn't ever seem to
make me feel whole.

ESCAPE

Where the calmness resides,
where the sun and moon dictate the tides,
where the scent of salt water soaks the air,
where my skin can be wet and bare,
where the sand gets in between my toes,
where I don't experience any lows,
this will be my favorite escape.

TAKING CONTROL

It's taken me
over two decades
to deal with my
demons,
the ones that make
me react and say
things I don't mean.
I despise them
sometimes,
but I despise myself more
for having a hard time
controlling them,
controlling me.

SET ME FREE

I don't belong
to anyone,
just as I don't
belong to myself.
My body belongs
to this earth
and my spirit
to the skies.

CLOSING THE CHAPTER

I am tired,
tired of writing
about you and how
all these pages
go on and on
about the hurt.
So, I'm closing that
chapter I allowed
you to write.

RESCUED

I
abandoned
love
to
save
myself.

LESSONS

She learned
to control
her temper
and her
mad silence
like an
art form.

SHEDDING

Every night
I slip off my skin,
pour my words
onto paper,
so I can
coexist in this
lonely world.

The Raven Flies at Midnight

Acknowledgments

I want to thank Christina Hart for putting up with all my changes, and for the endless hours of editing on her end. She has brought out something in me that I didn't think I had, and encouraged me to continue writing this book.
I also want to thank my dear friend Monika, who urged me to open an Instagram account after I told her that I used to love writing growing up but that I hadn't written in a very long time. Throughout a friendship that has lasted for more than 20 years, she has been someone who has stuck around for all my ups and downs.

Cover Design/Editing: Kat Savage & Christina Hart of Savage Hart Book Services

Kat Savage is an author and freelance graphic designer. She holds a degree in graphic design and advertising. To date, three of her books have topped an Amazon Hot New Releases list and Bestsellers list, including: *Learning To Speak, Mad Woman,* and *Anchors & Vacancies.*

Email:
katsavage@savagehartbookservices.com
Instagram: kat.savage

Christina Hart is an author and freelance editor. She has a BA in Creative Writing and English. To date, three of her books have been on Amazon Bestseller lists, including: *Empty Hotel Rooms Meant for Us, Letting Go Is an Acquired Taste,* and *Fresh Skin.*

Email:
christinahart@savagehartbookservices.com
Instagram: christinakaylenhart

Together, Savage and Hart created Savage Hart Book Services. With Savage's skill in design, and Hart's eye for editing, they partnered together on a mission to make self-published books just as polished and professional as traditionally published books, and maybe even a bit better.

www.savagehartbookservices.com
info@savagehartbookservices.com

Interior Artist: Tanja Weidenbörner

Tanja Weidenbörner is a modern self-taught artist who currently works and lives in Germany. Her paintings are based on thought, emotion, mental state, memory, lifestyle, and inner conflicts (never photos printed on canvas). She specializes in enamel paint and charcoal on canvas.

www.tw-artgallery.com

About the Author

Blackbird Poet is married and has two kids and a rescue dog. Currently, she resides in Roseville, CA, in one of the many places she's lived in from Southern California to Northern California. Her hope is that one day her final destination will be by the ocean, allowing the waves to lull her to sleep at night. This is her first published poetry collection. The origin of Blackbird Poet first came about to give her anonymity, when she decided on the name from a Nina Simone song. Within six months of opening up her Instagram account, she became public and started using her real name but still wanted to be referred to by her pseudonym.

Message to You

I can't begin to thank you enough for buying my book. It's still surreal to me that I have produced something that people actually want to read. For comments and/or questions, please feel free to contact me via email, Facebook, or Instagram, at:

Email: blackbirdpoetess@gmail.com
Facebook: blackbirdpoet
Instagram: blackbird.poet

Made in the USA
Middletown, DE
04 July 2017